Champions of the Animal World

Written by Keith Pigdon
Series Consultant: Linda Hoyt

WorldWise™
Content-based Learning

Contents

Introduction

A champion is a person who can do something better than anyone else. In all human sports, there are people who are champions.

There are also animal champions. They can swim, run, jump, dive and fly better than any other species of animal. They have special talents that help them get their food and not get eaten by **predators**.

Although these animal champions can escape from other animals, humans can be their most dangerous enemy. Many are or have been **threatened** by human activity.

Chapter 1

On the land

The cheetah

The cheetah is the fastest-running land animal over short distances. It can sprint at 100 **kilometres per hour** over 400 metres. Cheetahs use their amazing speed to catch their **prey**.

A cheetah has a light body and long legs. It has large nostrils that take in a lot of air. A cheetah's eyes are near the top of its head so that it can see its prey when it is running. A cheetah can bend its spine so that it can take very long strides when it runs.

Cheetahs are under threat because their habitat is being destroyed, and some are being captured and sold as pets.

They live on the plains of Africa.

Find out more

Find out about where cheetahs live.

The impala

Running and jumping over barriers is called **hurdling**. The impala is the hurdles champion of the animal world.

An impala can sprint at 80 kilometres per hour over 400 metres and leaps in the air as it runs. It can leap more than three metres high and more than ten metres across. An impala has a light body and long legs.

It uses its hurdling ability to escape **predators** such as lions. Lions cannot change direction as quickly as impalas, and they cannot leap in the air to catch impalas.

Impalas live on the plains of Africa.

Did you know?

The Olympic sprint champion runs at around 32 kilometres per hour over 400 metres.

The rocket frog

The rocket frog is the champion long jumper of the animal world.

It can jump more than 80 times its body length. A rocket frog has long, slender legs and very large feet.

Rocket frogs use their amazing long jumps to catch insects and other small animals. They also leap to safety when animals that prey on them come too close.

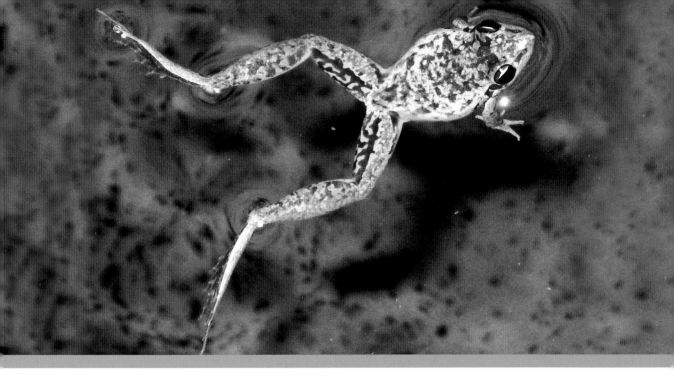

Many kinds of frogs are **threatened** because humans are draining swamps and waterways, and because less rain is falling in the swamps and ponds where frogs live.

Rocket frogs are found in Central America and Australia.

Did you know?

Olympic champions can jump four to five times their own body length.

Chapter 2
In the ocean

The sperm whale

The sperm whale is the champion diver of the animal world.

It dives deeper than any other animal.

Sperm whales dive 2,440 metres to find their favourite food, the giant squid. Sperm whales can hold their breath for more than one hour. This is much longer than other animals that breathe air, and it is why they can dive in the deep to catch giant squid.

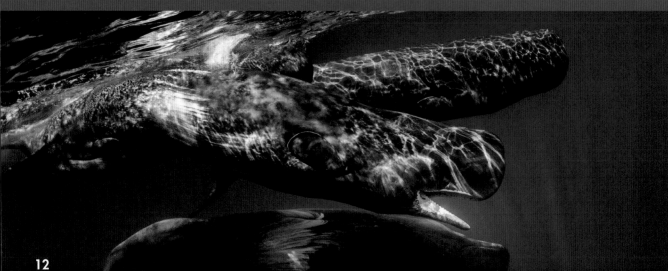

They were once **threatened** by too much whaling, but sperm whales are now protected, and their numbers are increasing.

Sperm whales live in the deepest parts of the ocean.

Find out more

What other animals that breathe air can dive to great depths?

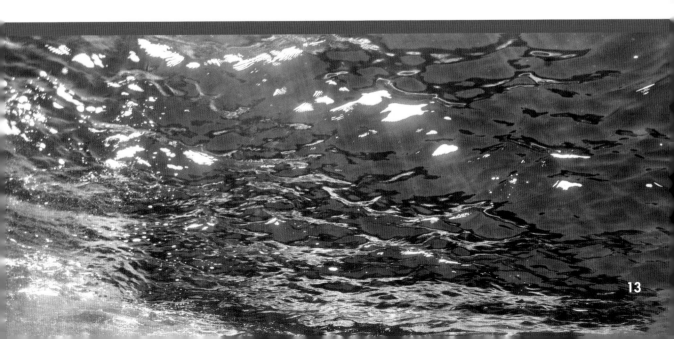

The sailfish

The sailfish is the champion swimmer of the animal world.

It can swim at 105 **kilometres per hour**.

Sailfish have a long, large back fin to help them swim fast. They have slim bodies with strong muscles that power their tails.

Sailfish use their speed to hunt schools of small fish, squid and octopus. Sometimes, humans **hunt** these fish for sport and food.

Sailfish are found in the Atlantic, Indian and Pacific Oceans.

Did you know?
The Olympic swimming champion swims 100 metres at about eight kilometres per hour.

Chapter 3

In the air

The peregrine falcon

The peregrine falcon reaches faster speeds than any other bird. It does this by flying very quickly and increasing its speed by diving from great heights.

In a dive, it can reach speeds of up to 280 **kilometres per hour**.

The peregrine falcon uses its flying and diving speeds to hit and stun its prey. It feeds on many kinds of smaller birds.

Fifty years ago, peregrine falcons were an **endangered** species. At that time, poisons that kill insects were widely used. Since then, these dangerous poisons have been banned and the peregrine falcon population has recovered.

Peregrine falcons are found all over the world.

Find out more
Why did insect poison endanger peregrine falcons?

Conclusion

Among all the animals on Earth, there are some that are **outstanding** in the things that they can do.

These animals have special talents that they use throughout their lives. Some use their talents to help them get food. Others use their talents to make sure **predators** do not eat them.

On the land, in the ocean, in lakes and ponds, and in the air they are champions of the animal world.

Glossary

endangered	to be at high risk of becoming extinct
hunt	to chase and kill an animal for food
hurdling	jumping over a solid object
kilometres per hour	the number of kilometres that would be travelled in one hour if the speed remained the same
outstanding	excellent or exceptional
predators	animals that hunt other animals for food
prey	animals that are hunted for food
threatened	to be at risk of becoming endangered

Index